THE WEALTH ASSAULT ON BOOMERS

How the government destroys your wealth through RMDs and estate taxes

STEVE EARL

ISBN 978-0-615-95362-5

Printed in the United States

Published by PSS Publishing
4227 Lafayette Center Drive
Chantilly, VA 20151

Due to the time-sensitive nature of the material in this book and the continuously changing IRS tax codes, all data including charts, worksheets, and tax information are for illustrative purposes only. You should consult your tax advisor and financial planner for information pertaining to your circumstance.

CONTENTS

Chapter 1

The Government Assault on Your Wealth

A person's lifetime can be measured by many different yardsticks. One measurement might take into account one's family achievements: a long and productive marriage, children that have been raised into successful adults, or the number of grandchildren that will carry with them the family's heritage. Another yardstick may be the professional achievements made over an entire career: a lawyer's partnership in the firm, a professor's tenure, an architect's portfolio of structures, and even a philanthropist's effect on his or her community. No matter what yardstick is used to measure a person's lifetime achievements, most people share one common thread through the courses of their lives. We all start out working hard to insure a more fruitful future.

My definition of work is not restricted to the hours spent in adulthood trading time for income. In work I include the twelve years we spend in school as children and the years we spend as young adults in universities, trade schools, and professional continuing education courses to advance our careers—all in addition to the forty years we each spend working in our chosen trades.

No matter what yardstick we use to measure our successes, by the time we achieve late adulthood, all of us have built up a long resume of work. With a little (or a lot of) diligence and a bit of fortune, in late adulthood we also have greater financial independence, the choice to pursue a preferred trade, and the ability to leave a legacy to successive family generations. You most likely achieved financial independence through mastering your trade, building a successful business, and/or years of deferred consumption (better known as savings and investing). Probably, a combination of all of these continues to contribute to your financial independence.

You probably created your successful business, professional practice, and career or investment strategy without much thought about federal incentives. Assets such as real estate, jewelry, or precious metals probably complement a portfolio of stocks, bonds, and other income-producing investments. And if you own a business or plan to continue to engage in your occupation, the need for additional income is probably not a concern.

Up to this point, your financial planning has served you well, and your thoughts are more likely geared toward preserving your assets and minimizing taxes. What you may not have realized is the inevitable financial disruption in your near future (if it has not already started).

Looming within everyone's portfolio are two

types of assets that for years have been camouflaged as an insurance against the income loss of aging. Unfortunately, the deferred cost of these social insurance assets comes with strong financial repercussions for anyone that continues to produce income during the typical years of retirement.

One of these assets is your Social Security benefit. Social Security requirements mandate that taxable distributions be taken by age 70, whether you need the income or not. Not only are the distributions taxable, but they can also increase the marginal tax rate you pay on existing income because they add to your taxable income. The effect could be significant, as the 2013 tax laws have not only increased marginal tax rates but also created a new tax surcharge on investment income.

The distribution requirements are not just limited to Social Security. They also include a second type of asset: most tax-qualified retirement savings accounts. Many sponsored retirement savings accounts are subject to taxable required minimum distributions

(RMDs) after you reach age 70½. These distributions also have the negative impact of being taxable and increasing your marginal tax rate in addition to potentially subjecting your investment income to the new tax surcharge.

Like most hardworking Americans, you have built your financial independence not as a result of federally sponsored savings plans, but in spite of them. The taxes you have paid into the Social Security system over your lifetime could probably have been used more productively, and the ensuing required benefit distributions may not be needed. This is a fast-growing challenge that many baby boomers are facing. The programs intended to provide a safety net for lower-income workers have not only required you to pay a lifetime income tax under the Federal Insurance Contributions Act (FICA), but now also require you to take taxable distributions, further devaluing your net worth and the assets passed on to your heirs.

The Government Safety Net

The promise of financial independence is made to all Americans, courtesy of the federal government, via tax-*favored* (more accurately defined as "pay Uncle Sam more later") retirement plans and Social Security. The latter, the Social Security Act signed by Franklin Delano Roosevelt in 1935 and put into effect in 1937, is recognized by all Americans each pay period in the form of FICA tax. The exact effects of FICA are currently 6.2% tax paid by the employee and 6.2% paid by the employer, for a total of 12.4% of your paycheck. In return, each taxpaying American may elect to receive a retirement benefit starting at age 62, with mandatory withdrawal at age 70.

Having never intended for Social Security to be the primary savings vehicle for Americans, Congress later enacted additional laws to encourage savings. And although federally acknowledged retirement plans predate 1974, it was the Employee Retirement Income Security Act of 1974 that first authorized the individual retirement account (IRA) to encourage retirement savings. An IRA allowed everyone, including individuals without employer-sponsored plans, to have retirement savings accounts with the same tax deferral benefits of employer plans. Shortly afterward, the Revenue Act of 1978 included a provision for the Internal Revenue Code (IRC) now known as Section 401(k), which allowed employees to defer receipt of income, and therefore taxes owed on it, to age 59½ (up to age 70½).

These laws passed in the last century, intending to stimulate savings while providing a financial security net for lower-income workers, have done little to benefit the middle to upper working classes in America. For them, the Social Security tax on wages equal to 12.4% of income imposes a far greater cost than the potential benefits. For example, based upon 2013 FICA taxes, a worker earning the maximum taxable FICA limit of $113,700 will pay a combined employee/employer tax of $14,098. If everything else remained constant, over a 40-year working life, the $14,098 invested at 6% interest would be worth $2.1 million. This is far more than what this worker can expect back in Social Security benefits. Even more disturbing is the fact that benefits you earn based upon taxes paid over your lifetime cannot be classified as an asset you own outright. Social Security benefits are only provided to you during your living years, and with the exception of widower benefits, payments do not continue to your estate. That means that for many Americans, taxes paid into the system will never be realized back for either the payer or his or her family.

It's not that the tax deferral incentives of retirement accounts are bad and should be ignored by everyone. In fact, for many low-wage workers, the incentives of tax deferral and employer matching contribution plans are a good supplement to the Social Security system. It does exactly what it was designed to do: create a safety net for low-wage workers who would probably not have had the opportunity to save adequate retirement funds otherwise. That said, those who find themselves at the middle-to-upper end of the wage scale face steep taxes and penalties, which are used to subsidize the social benefits system.

IRA/401(k): The Tax Shelter Myth

The tax-favored retirement vehicles we have add little value to a middle class worker's hopes for funding retirement. Given the low maximum contribution limits of IRA/401(k)s, it is even less likely that a meaningful retirement can be created using them. For example, given the 2013 IRA maximum contribution limit of $5,500, a 40-year investment at 6% would have resulted in $850,000 of account value (only $550,000 after taxes). Not a bad little sum of money, but hardly enough for a full retirement. And if you think that the tax-deferred status of the IRA makes it more attractive, then consider the fact that the same $5,500 (or roughly $3,575 after taxes) invested at 6% would still return close to the same $550,000 after 40 years. It makes very little difference whether you pay Uncle Sam's tax up front or defer it until later.

Odds are, you may not have given it much thought—but you already realize these facts.

Your ability to pass assets to your heirs and avoid devaluing your net worth rests on understanding the social benefits system of the federal government and the underlying tax needs of Uncle Sam. The price of improper planning can be devastating. Half of your net worth can quickly get consumed by taxes as required distributions are taken. Remember, the required minimum distributions from retirement accounts serve as a source of tax revenue for Uncle Sam. Fortunately there are extremely effective tools that can reverse the negative impact of RMDs while amplifying the benefits passed to heirs. Your ability to leverage required distributions can create a financial estate plan that works not only to maximize the assets you pass to your heirs, but to allow you to pay your heirs tax free. But passing those hard-earned assets to loved ones requires understanding more than a brief overview of the impact distributions can have on an estate. It is equally important to understand and address the less obvious challenges everyone must face to assure the preservation of assets.

Don't be fooled into thinking that these laws

and tax codes do not apply to you, or that you will somehow find an exemption. The social benefit systems created by the federal government and the tax codes enacted to fund them are not just history. They universally impact Americans today. The present discussion is material to anyone that plans on leaving assets to a spouse, children, charity, or any other cause. Your lifetime of achievement obligates you to address these issues. Learn the strategies in these pages to combat the dilution of your assets.

Chapter 2

RMD: The Three-Letter Word

By definition, a distribution is the allotment or dilution of an item. In itself, receiving a distribution or the gradual liquidation of an asset should cause little concern. Assuming the asset does not lose value, distributing it into another form need not have a negative effect. For example, if you had $10,000 in a mutual fund and decided to take a full distribution of it, you would have $10,000 in cash. The distribution simply changed the form of your asset from mutual fund to cash; it did not change the value.

Now imagine that your $10,000 in cash is sitting in your bank account. Most likely, you decide to keep the money there because you can distribute the money into other investments at the same value. If the distribution from the mutual fund were to cost you a tax of half your asset's value, it is highly unlikely that you would have transferred it. Why would anyone deposit $10,000 into an account if they could only ever take out $6,000?

We all assume that if we have $10,000 in a bank, we own an asset valued at $10,000. Now let's assume that the $10,000 sitting in the bank is classified as an IRA. Like most, you would probably also count it as a $10,000 asset. We tend to consider all our investments to be worth the current value of the underlying asset. Seldom do we consider its true distributed value. We make this error because we are used to accepting distributions as exchange of assets from one form to another in equal value. Therein lies the problem. It is not the distribution itself, but the consequence of the distribution, that affects an asset's value. And in most situations, there is very little, if any, consequence to a distribution; therefore, we mentally assign most assets their full values.

Unfortunately, not all distributions are created equal. In fact, as we get older—particularly after age 60—many of our assets have severe distribution penalties. The most obvious example of this is the estate tax (or "death tax," as many call it). When you die, your estate may pay over 40% in federal taxes before distributions to heirs can be made. The estate tax is simply the final stage of the distribution tax system. The beginning stages are in Social Security and tax-favored retirement plans. The distribution requirements of tax-favored plans such as your IRA/401(k) are nothing more than a forced tax on assets. They require you to liquidate your retirement accounts, in effect devaluing them as assets by up to 50%.

The distribution most penalized is your Social Security payment. This account has the heaviest burden in that all distributions are subject to income taxes, and in that the value of future payments are completely lost upon death. At least with an IRA/401(k) plan, any remaining value after distributions can be left to your heirs. The distribution penalties of Social Security seem harsh, considering the fact that your account is distributing back to you money you were required to pay into the system through years of FICA taxes. All of these stages of the distribution tax system, prefaced by RMDs, take a significant toll on the value of an estate.

RMDs Revealed

Required minimum distributions are the minimum amounts that a qualified retirement plan owner must withdraw, usually no later than age 70½. A plan owner that does not withdraw the required amount on time faces high penalties. The requirement for withdrawal does not end with the owner's life either; the surviving spouse must then take withdrawals or be subject to penalties. Remember, RMDs are as much a tax revenue generator for Uncle Sam as they are a social benefits system for lower-wage workers. Their effects are to end tax deferrals on investment accounts and raise marginal tax rates while extracting tax revenue—and all of this before any remaining amounts are subjected to estate taxes.

Social Security benefits and their required payout are also a form of RMD. You are required to begin receiving Social Security benefits no later than age 70. These benefits add to your Adjusted Gross Income (AGI), often pushing you into the next higher marginal tax bracket. In addition to an increase in your marginal tax rate, the Net Investment Income tax put into effect January 1, 2013, requires an additional 3.8% tax on most investment income, including but not limited to interest, dividends, capital gains, and rental income on Adjusted Gross Income of $200,000 for individuals and $250,000 for those married filing jointly.

RMDs effectively work to liquidate a person's retirement account assets before death. The required distribution counts as additional taxable income to the account owner. The purpose, of course, is to raise tax revenue from the account. For IRA/401(k) owners with existing income, it creates more tax revenue for Uncle Sam by elevating the owner's marginal tax rate. If an owner predeceases a spouse, the IRA/401(k) account can be transferred to the surviving spouse without tax penalty under the unlimited estate marital deduction. Any distributions from the plan then fall under the surviving spouse's tax bracket, which could be significantly lower. This is the best-casc scenario. If there is no surviving spouse and the IRA/401(k) account causes the owner's federal and state tax exemption to be exceeded, it would generate an estate tax.

The worst possible trap that you must avoid is having your heirs rely on the value of the IRA/401(k) account to pay your estate's taxes. If your heirs need to withdraw money from the IRA/401(k) to do that, they will have to pay income tax on the distribution in addition to the estate tax itself. In this way, your heirs could effectively lose anywhere from 50% to 90% of the account's value to taxes.

The effects of RMDs are easy to see when comparing marginal tax rates before and after exposure to an RMD.

In ***Example 1***, Bob, age 68, is married and works as an architect for a small firm. He continues to work, drawing a salary of $175,000 and has unearned investment income of $45,000. This would place him in a marginal tax bracket of 28% and not subject to the new investment income surtax. However, by age 70 he draws Social Security payments and takes the RMD from his IRA/401(k). On the surface, Bob's actual $220,000 earnings only increase by the addition of Social Security payments, since the income gained from his IRA/401(k) accounts caused an equal reduction of their account value: Bob had $905,000 in combined IRA/401(k) value, and his first distribution simply reduced it by $33,000.

It's hard to consider a distribution real income if it is your own money. Yet, due to Social Security payments plus distributions from his IRA/401(k), Bob's AGI increased to $291,000, moving his marginal tax bracket up to 33%. And, all of his investment income is now subject to a 3.8% surtax, since his total tax bracket exceeds $250,000. The combination puts his effective marginal tax rate at 36.8%.

Example 1

Bob's Earned Salary: $175,000
Unearned Investment Income: $45,000

IRA Value: $385,000
401(k) Value: $520,000
Non-Qualified Investment Accounts: $525,000
Real Estate Assets: $1,150,000

Effect of RMD on Bob's Income and Marginal Tax Rate

	Current Age 68	**After RMD at Age 70**
Earned Income	$175,000	$175,000
Unearned Income (Dividends, Interest, Rent)	$45,000	$45,000
IRA/401(k) Required Distribution (Asset value divided by 27.4)	n/a	$33,000
Social Security Benefits	n/a	$38,000
Total Adjusted Gross Income	$220,000	$291,000
Marginal Tax Bracket	**28%**	33%
Investment Income Surtax	0%	3.8%
Total Tax on Investment Income		**36.8%**

Accounts that Fall under the RMD Rules

RMD rules apply to any employer-sponsored retirement plan, including 401(k), 403(b), 457(b), and profit-sharing plans. IRAs, SIMPLE IRAs, SEPs, and SARSEPs are also included. Essentially, if the plan was funded with pretax dollars, RMD rules apply. Roth IRAs are not covered by RMD rules, as their contributions are made with after-tax dollars.

Calculating RMDs

Each year, starting no later than age 70½, an owner of an account subject to an RMD must calculate the minimum distribution and make the withdrawal by the required deadline. The first RMD withdrawal must be taken by April 1 of the year you turn 70½. Thereafter, each RMD withdrawal must occur no later than December 31.

You calculate the required distribution of each account type subject to the rules by dividing its total value at the beginning of withdrawals by the number of distribution years. You can add the values of the same type, such as two IRA accounts, and then take the required distribution from a single IRA, but you cannot group account values from different types. For example, you can't add up the value of a 401(k) and an IRA and then make a distribution from the 401(k) only. If you have many different types of accounts, then each year, you need to make separate calculations by account type and take the appropriate distributions from each type. Failure to take the required minimum distribution is subject to an excise tax of up to 50% on the amount not distributed as required.

Example 2 illustrates how Bob calculates his RMD and concludes that he needs to take a distribution of $14,051 from his IRA and $18,978 from an existing 401(k).

Example 2

Distribution period from Uniform Lifetime Table: 27.4

IRA balance on December 31 of prior year: $385,000

IRA balance ***divided by*** distribution period = **$14,051**

401(k) balance on December 31 of prior year: $520,000

401(k) balance ***divided by*** distribution period = **$18,978**

Bob's RMD Calculation

	Account Value	Distribution Period	RMD
IRA Balance	$385,000	27.4	$14,051
401(k) Balance	$520,000	27.4	$18,978

Effect of RMDs on Your Heirs

Even if we accept the premise that Social Security and RMDs have a positive overall effect on our society by generating tax revenue for our government, we cannot dispute the negative impact that wealth redistribution has on our heirs. The consequences to heirs do not apply just to the wealthy few subject to estate tax thresholds, but to everyone that has paid a FICA tax or saved money in a qualified retirement plan.

What most people fail to consider is that Social Security payments have considerable value while they are alive. Ten years of Social Security payments to someone receiving $38,000 annually (our friend Bob, for example) adds up to $380,000 (and $760,000 after 20 years). These benefits can be enjoyed by children and grandchildren in the form of gifts while the Social Security recipient is alive. But when the recipient dies, the payments stop and the account value goes to zero.

If you believe the value of the account goes

to a surviving spouse in the form of survivor benefits, you are almost correct: a surviving spouse, however, can only keep one set of benefits. To keep the deceased spouse's benefits, he or she must give up his or her own—or vice versa. Either way, one set of benefits is lost. The loss of these benefits has a real and measurable effect on the value of an estate. Those lucky enough to live long lives can convert Social Security payments into tangible assets that can be left to heirs.

While Bob is alive and collecting Social Security payments, he can convert those payments into gifts to his children and grandchildren. And although RMDs will reduce the value of his IRA and 401(k), at least their remaining value can still be passed on to his heirs after his death.

Example 3 illustrates how the value of Bob's estate assets is greatly destroyed with the loss of Social Security and the application of RMD taxes. His current value of Social Security benefits and retirement accounts are $1,425,000. After RMD taxes at his marginal tax rate of 36.8% and the end of Social Security benefits at death, his heirs will only receive $571,960. Bob's heirs will lose almost two-thirds of the value of assets passed on after Bob's death, not taking into consideration any potential federal or state estate taxes.

Example 3

The Erosion of Bob's Estate

	Current Value of Assets	Post RMD Value of Assets to Heirs	Loss
401(k)	$520,000	$328,640	-$191,360
IRA	$385,000	$243,320	-$141,680
Social Security (x 10 Years)	$380,000	$ 0	-$380,000
Total	**$1,425,000**	**$571,960**	**-$853,040**

Chapter 3

RMD Strategies

It is easy to see how the effects of RMDs can quickly reduce the value of assets. Years of saving and investing are quickly compromised as taxes eat away at investment returns. Even the best-planned portfolios can suffer inadvertent slowdown in growth as marginal tax rates increase. And without the proper planning, your heirs may be forced to make heavily taxed withdrawals from inherited retirement accounts just to pay federal and state estate taxes. In as short as ten years from the moment you are age 70, the assets that you worked hard to accumulate over a lifetime can be reduced 50 to 75%, leaving very little legacy to your heirs.

Taking Back What You Lost

Fortunately, there are some unique tools and strategies, widely available but known of by few, to combat the impact of RMDs. These tools can not only use life expectancy to reverse the liquidating effects of RMDs but also leverage the required distributions to greatly amplify the benefits to your estate.

The tools for undoing the damage caused by RMDs are life insurance and annuities.Very few people, including even financial advisors, understand how the tax-favored benefits of life insurance properly utilized can offset the liquidating effects RMDs have on your wealth. Life insurance is the only tool available that can take one dollar of premium and turn it into many dollars of tax-free benefit to your heirs. It is one of the few tools that bypasses the expense of probate and passes the money directly to your heirs or estate, and life insurance benefits are generally not subject to taxes. This means that you can pass 100% of your life insurance policy benefits to your heirs, tax free.

The ability to pass benefits tax free to your heirs enables you to cost-effectively recover the value lost to RMD taxes and ending Social Security benefits. Best of all, any unneeded Social Security benefits or RMDs can be used to fund an RMD life insurance strategy. Relative to the benefits received, the cost of life insurance is small. An average, guaranteed-for-life policy for a 70-year-old male can easily take a dollar of annual premium and turn it into 30 dollars of benefits. This large multiplying effect makes life insurance the most affordable solution for asset preservation.

Reversing Taxes Paid on RMDs

Federal and state income taxes can shrink a retirement account value by more than 50% once all the RMDs have been taken. As we've seen, this leaves very little behind for heirs. If you fund a life insurance plan with a portion of the RMD, your retirement portfolio can guarantee back to the heirs all taxes lost over the distribution lifetime. This works well for any retirement plan that is subjected to taxes and/or penalties. Remember, in the case of IRA/401(k)s and other qualified plans, your heirs will also be subject to income taxes on distributions made to them. Choosing the proper life insurance benefit amount ensures that the estate taxes on the IRA/401(k) are paid, avoiding the costly need to liquidate the IRA/401(k) prematurely. Insurance benefits received in excess of the estate tax bill due on the IRA/401(k) will help your heirs pay the income taxes on further distributions.

The Social Security Gotcha

As I've noted, Social Security is an insurance program created to secure the retirement needs of low-wage workers. The benefits you receive are probably never going to equal the tax dollars you spent funding the plan over your working life. And worst of all, of course, when a Social Security recipient dies, his or her benefits stop, or at best get transferred to the surviving spouse. (In any case, he or she loses the lower paying of the possible two benefits, even though years of taxes were paid.) And although your family may not need the Social Security benefits today, the loss of your current income may make the otherwise surplus Social Security benefits seem very valuable. It's not exactly a fair system, but it was never meant to be.

Once again, the benefits of funding a life insurance strategy with either an RMD or Social Security benefits are apparent. If your spouse and/or family were no longer able to enjoy the income you provide, such insurance can replace the lost value of your Social Security benefits while assuring that years of FICA payments are not lost. Your heirs would also enjoy the full value of your retirement accounts and have proper funds to pay taxes due on any proceeds from those accounts.

Looking back at *Example 3*, Bob can recover all the lost value of ending Social Security benefits and RMD taxes with an $850,000

RMD life insurance strategy.

Your Ability to Combat RMDs

Your ability to combat RMDs is contingent upon one factor above all others: your health. It underlies your ability to obtain an effective life insurance policy because its costs and benefits are proportional to life expectancy. It is extremely important to protect your insurability, since you are leveraging against your life expectancy to receive the best spread between premiums and benefits. If you are still a few years away from your age 70 RMDs, you must without hesitation protect your ability to combat their future effects.

Remember, required minimum distributions are a certainty that no one can avoid. Like death and taxes, RMDs are lurking right around the corner. The good news is that you can protect your ability to counter RMDs by purchasing a life insurance policy in advance of retirement. Locking in rates and coverage at a younger age is always more advantageous than waiting.

If price is a concern and you want to defer more expensive permanent coverage until RMDs can fund the plan, then a low-cost term life insurance plan is a great option. Term allows you to lock in rates while you are younger and the status of your health is known. Term insurance is relatively inexpensive and can be purchased in time periods to match the point at which you will need a more permanent RMD insurance solution. The most important part of this strategy is to make sure that your term policy offers guaranteed conversion into a quality permanent life insurance plan.

Annuity Strategy

An annuity is a contract with an insurance company: you deposit a sum of money with it, and in return, the company pays you interest on the deposit—not unlike a savings account. The annuity contract then allows you to liquidate the value of the account over a selected period. It is the withdrawal of the money that makes annuity contracts unique: you specify a guaranteed period of withdrawals up to lifetime. Annuities can be a great option for holding IRA or retirement funds. Annuities can receive tax-qualified funds without penalty, allowing for easy transfers of existing retirement accounts into a new annuity.

Using an annuity as a retirement account gives the owner great flexibility when it comes time to fund an RMD life insurance strategy. When the RMD is due, the annuity can begin payout directly into a life insurance policy. This enables the owner to avoid making manual payments and potential lapses in coverage. Since annuities offer the flexibility of guaranteed lifetime payments, there is never fear that changing market conditions could prematurely liquidate an account and leave the life insurance strategy unfunded.

Chapter 4

Insurance Plan Types

There's no shortage of life insurance plan types that can defend you against RMDs. If you are already at the RMD age, the best choice is a permanent life insurance plan that has guaranteed premiums and guaranteed death benefits for life. This ensures that your insurance plan matches the duration of your RMDs. For those with a few years before RMDs begin, it is imperative to protect your ability to buy the proper insurance. This is best accomplished with low-cost term insurance. These simple but effective products are widely available from financial advisors.

Whole Life

Whole life insurance policies offer death benefit guarantees for life and a guaranteed, level premium. Whole life policies also have a cash value that can be liquidated if the policy is no longer needed. Due to the inherent guarantees of death benefit, premium costs, and cash value, these plans tend to be the most expensive, offering a lower death-benefit-to-premium ratio. By design, whole life plans offer less flexibility for changes. Since the cash accumulation component of whole life policies is not needed in RMD planning, a lower-cost insurance plan is often preferable.

Guaranteed Universal Life

Universal life insurance policies have become a popular alternative to traditional whole life insurance plans. Like whole life plans, universal life plans offer a death benefit in exchange for a premium payment while accumulating an internal cash value. Traditional universal life policies sacrificed guaranteed premiums and guaranteed death benefits in exchange for higher interest payments on the policy cash value. In recent years, the popularity of universal life, in part due to its flexibility, has created hybrid policies that act very much like whole life plans while minimizing the cash accumulation component. These guaranteed premium universal life plans offer the premium and death benefit guarantees of whole life at a reduced cost. Guaranteed premium universal life plans are the preferred choice for RMD planning. Owners can reduce their overall cost of insurance, maximizing their premium-to-benefit ratio while enjoying all the needed guarantees.

Guaranteed Level Term

For those not already at the RMD age, I've noted that term insurance can serve in the interim. Term insurance can be a very cost-effective way to lock in coverage at your current health status so that a future permanent insurance plan is guaranteed. Term life insurance plans offer an exchange of death benefit for premium without the added expense of a cash value. Term plans can be typically purchased with term lengths of 1 to 30 years, depending on your age. Guaranteed level term plans keep both the death benefit and premiums level for the contract period.

For RMD planning, it is imperative that the guaranteed level term plan has guaranteed conversion privileges. Guaranteed conversion is a policy clause allowing you to exchange the term coverage for permanent coverage, without proof of insurability, during the term period. This is crucial, since the purpose of the term is to ensure that you have a permanent RMD insurance solution when you need it. This is why I highly recommend that your plan come from a reputable insurance company that has quality permanent insurance policies.

Do not be persuaded simply by prices. Many low-cost term insurance providers may not have competitive permanent products, thus making their term plans inadequate for your future RMD planning needs. Consider not only price but the insurance company's existing permanent products and their history of offering such plans.

Note that since the actual permanent policy available in the future may be unknown, buying term insurance may not guarantee a successful future RMD life insurance strategy. This approach should be used with caution and an understanding of the potential risks.

Chapter 5

A Simple Solution

Responsibility, hard work, persistence, and planning are the words we most often use to describe a successful person's lifetime of achievements. It is the years of diligently exercising those traits that enables successful people to build wealth. Although motivations may vary, for most, the underlying theme that drives success is the desire to provide a better life for their loved ones. But the desire to provide for loved ones does not end at retirement, and certainly not at death. A lifetime of achievement also empowers us to leave a lasting legacy to our heirs.

The American dream to provide a better life and greater opportunities to our future generations is a cornerstone of our culture. We grow up with these principles in mind and apply them throughout our work lives. We pride ourselves on giving everyone equal opportunity for success and lending a hand to our neighbors so that they may also achieve the American dream. Unfortunately, the same laws intended to provide a safety net to those less fortunate create large penalties and tax burdens for others. The need for Uncle Sam to finance the social savings programs through taxes and wealth redistribution is in direct conflict with the premise of working to provide a better life for our heirs. Combating the increasing taxes and wealth redistribution mechanisms is vital to provide your lasting legacy.

The effects of RMDs can reduce your retirement account value more than 50%, and estate taxes can shrink the wealth left to heirs by as much as 90%. The impact of RMDs on marginal tax rates can cause an increased tax burden on existing ordinary income and subject you to the additional investment surtax. The combination of RMD requirements and their resulting tax implications, along with federal estate taxes, ultimately act as a wealth redistribution tool for Uncle Sam. These wealth redistribution taxes imposed on everyone make it difficult to pass the full value of your wealth to heirs.

RMDs and estate taxes can be equalized with the use of a life insurance strategy. The wealth loss due to the increase in marginal tax rates can be reversed, and the destructive impact on estate taxes can be eliminated. These simple but lesser-known strategies do not require expensive consultants and can be implemented by anyone. The only prerequisite to success is action.

As I have stressed, your ability to execute on an RMD life insurance strategy rests on your ability to obtain a life insurance policy. If you are a few years away from RMD requirements, then prioritize securing a life insurance term policy. If you are already subjected to RMDs, then it is imperative that you stop the loss immediately and reverse the effects on your heirs. Acquiring a permanent life insurance plan that has guaranteed premiums and guaranteed death benefits for life ensures that your insurance plan matches the duration of your RMDs. This strategy prevents the destruction of your wealth and protects the legacy to your heirs you have worked so hard to build.

Appendix

Customize Your Strategy

The worksheets in the next few pages are designed to help you calculate the effects RMDs will have on you and your heirs. The *RMD Calculation Worksheet* allows you to determine the correct Distribution Period for your age and resulting RMD for your IRA/401(k) accounts. Using the *RMD Calculation Account Summary* you can add up all of your pension accounts and determine the correct distribution amount for each account type. Remember, you are required to calculate an RMD for each different account type, such as all IRA's or all 401(k) accounts. You may then take the required distribution from a single account of the same type.

The next worksheet, *RMD Effect of Marginal Tax Rates* will help you compare the before and after effects of RMDs on your marginal tax rates. This will help you determine the impact on your estate and ultimately on your heirs, as illustrated using the *RMD Effect on Estate worksheet*. The final calculation *The Insurance Needed to Recover RMD* Loss will give you an estimate of how much life insurance you need to assure a successful RMD insurance strategy.

Together all of these worksheets will help you prepare for RMDs in order to minimize their impact on your wealth.

RMD Calculation Worksheet
(For illustrative purposes only)

IRA balance on December 31 of previous year ________

Distribution period from Uniform Lifetime Table ________

IRA balance ***divided by*** distribution period = RMD _____

Repeat Calculation for each IRA/401(k)

Uniform Lifetime Table

For use by unmarried retirement account owners, married owners whose spouses are not more than 10 years younger, and married owners whose spouses are not the sole beneficiaries of their IRAs.

Data taken from 2013 Table III in *IRS Publication 590 (2012), Individual Retirement Arrangements (IRAs).*

AGE	RMD	AGE	RMD	AGE	RMD
70	27.4	80	18.7	90	11.4
71	26.5	81	17.9	91	10.8
72	25.6	82	17.1	92	10.2
73	24.7	83	16.3	93	9.6
74	23.8	84	15.5	94	9.1
75	22.9	85	14.8	95	8.6
76	22.0	86	14.1	96	8.1
77	21.2	87	13.4	97	7.6
78	20.3	88	12.7	98	7.1
79	19.5	89	12.0	99	6.7

RMD Calculation Account Summary

IRA	Account Value	Dist. Period	RMD
1			
2			
3			
Totals			

401(k)	Account Value	Dist. Period	RMD
1			
2			
3			
Totals			

Other	Account Value	Dist. Period	RMD
1			
2			
3			
Totals			
		Total Distributions	

RMD effect on Marginal Tax Rate

	Current Age	After RMD at Age 70
Earned Income		
Unearned Income (Dividends, Interest, Rent)		
IRA/401(k) Required Distributions (Asset value divided by 27.4)		
Social Security Benefits		
Total Adjusted Gross Income		
Marginal Tax Bracket		
Investment Income Surtax (if applicable)		
Total Tax on Investment Income		

RMD effect on Estate

	Current Value of your Assets	Post RMD Value of Assets to Heirs (Deduct loss from taxes)	Loss
401(k)			
IRA			
Social Security (x 10 Years)			
Total			

↓

Insurance needed to recover RMD loss	

2013 RMD Quick Chart

(IRAs vs. Defined Contribution Plans)

Basic RMD rules applying to IRAs and defined contribution plans (e.g., 401(k), profit-sharing, and 403(b) plans).

Required Minimum Distributions for Account Owners		
401(k)	IRAs including SEP, SIMPLE and SARSEP IRAs	Defined Contribution Plans
RMD Dates	You must take your first RMD by April 1 of the year following the year in which you turn 70½, regardless of whether you are still employed.	You must take your first RMD by April 1 of the year following the later of the year you turn 70½ or the year you retire (if allowed by your plan). If you are a 5% owner, you must start RMDs by April 1 of the year following the year you turn 70½.
When do I reach age 70½?	You reach age 70½ on the date 6 calendar months after your 70th birthday.	Same as IRA rule.
Calculating RMD	Dividing adjusted market value of IRAs as of December 31 of the preceding year by the distribution period that corresponds with your age in the Uniform Lifetime Table (Table III in IRS Publication 590 (2012), Individual Retirement Arrangements (IRAs)). If your spouse is your sole beneficiary and is more than 10 years younger than you, you will use the Joint Life and Last Survivor Expectancy Table (Table II in IRS Publication 590).	Same as IRA rule. Your plan sponsor/administrator should calculate the RMD for you.

May I take more than one withdrawal in a year to meet my RMD?	Yes.	Same as IRA rule.
What happens if I do not take the RMD?	Subject to an additional tax equal to 50% of the undistributed RMD.	Same as IRA rule.

Note: There are no RMD requirements for a Roth IRA while the owner is alive. However, designated Roth accounts are subject to the RMD rules.

2013 Federal Income Tax Brackets

Filing Individually:
- $0 to $8,925 = 10% rate
- $8,926 to $36,250 = 15%
- $36,251 to $87,850 = 25%
- $87,851 to $183,250 = 28%
- $183,251 to $398,350 = 33%
- $398,351 to $400,000 = 35%
- $400,001 and above = 39.6%

Married Filing Jointly:
- $0 to $17,850 = 10%
- $17,851 to $72,500 = 15%
- $72,501 to $146,400 = 25%
- $146,401 to $223,050 = 28%
- $223,051 to $398,350 = 33%
- $398,351 to $450,000 = 35%
- $450,001 and over = 39.6%

Married Filing Separately:
- $0 to $8925 = 10%
- $8,926 to $36,250 = 15%
- $36,251 to $73,200 = 25%
- $73,201 to $111,525 = 28%
- $111,526 to $199,175 = 33%
- $199,176 to $225,000 = 35%
- $225,001 and over = 39.6%

References

IRS Publication 590 (2012), Individual Retirement Arrangements (IRAs)

IRS Publication 15 (2013), (Circular E), Employer's Tax Guide

http://www.irs.gov/uac/Newsroom/Net-Investment-Income-Tax-FAQs

http://www.irs.gov/pub/irs-tege/uniform_rmd_wksht.pdf

http://www.ssa.gov/planners/benefitcalculators.htm

About the author

Steve Earl has worked in the financial services industry for over twenty years. His unique insight into personal finance has been developed through his experiences with consumers, small business owners, and professionals. As a business owner he has built a successful national financial services company and continues to speak around the country.